The arboretum is owned and managed by the Woodland Trust.

More than 10,000 young saplings were planted in 2015/16 by Heartwood volunteers.

The arboretum was planned with design input from forest landscape architect, Simon Bell.

Many of the descriptions have been taken directly from the Woodland Trust web site, www.woodlandtrust.org.uk. Other sources are acknowledged on page 46.

This book has been funded by the Woodland Trust and all profits will go directly to them for the management of their sites including Heartwood Forest.

Printed by The Ludo Press Ltd, 020 8879 1881,
www.ludo.co.uk

Published by Kate Bretherton 2017

Background photo: an aerial photo of the arboretum

Heartw Native

C000186289

By Brian I

Contents   Page

The Arboretum and British Woodland

Heartwood Arboretum

The Woodland Trust acquired 350 ha of land for Heartwood Forest in 2008 and began planting one of the largest, new, native forests in the UK. It includes 25 species typical of woodlands in Hertfordshire and is managed as a natural wild forest. In 2015 the Woodland Trust and a group of volunteers conceived the idea of planting an 11 ha arboretum of all sixty of the trees and shrubs native to the British Isles. It was planted in 2015-2016 and visitors can enjoy the beauty and diversity of our trees whilst learning about the ways in which they have been used over the centuries.

Native trees and shrubs

We define "native" to include only species that arrived after the last ice-age and before man had a major influence: that is roughly 10,000 - 3,000 BC. Many others have become naturalised and now grow and propagate in the wild; for example, sweet chestnut and walnut, which were brought by the Romans, and horse chestnut and sycamore, which arrived in the Middle Ages. In the arboretum we have planted only true natives. Our guiding reference is the list published by the Royal Horticultural Society (p 45) and the arboretum includes virtually all our trees and large and medium shrubs. Exceptions are some of the whitebeam (*Sorbus*) and rose (*Rosa*) species.

Trees as a valuable resource

Over the years ancient and native woodlands have been an essential source of timber, fuel, coppice products, food including venison, and other sustainable products. When woodland products were vital to our livelihood we knew how each species of tree could be used for different purposes, and how to grow for quality. For example, where trees were to be used for timber they were planted close together and selectively thinned to give long straight trunks. Wood became the feedstock of a vibrant artisan economy in which woodland was highly valued and nurtured.

Our woods today

Globalisation has led to a flood of imported products that are cheaper, and often preferred, to those produced by our native species. We now make wine from grapes rather than elderberries, jam from apricots in preference to rowan and hawthorn berries, and where once we might have eaten cherries from our native trees we now eat peaches and bananas. Most of our seasoned timber market is supplied by imports, and when we grow our own timber we often use exotic trees such as sitka spruce and lodgepole pine. Even the oak used in this country is nearly all imported. The British Isles now has only 1.3% of its area covered with ancient semi-natural woodland and most is unmanaged. Increasingly, however our woodlands are being recognised and valued for the more subtle yet vital environmental services they provide, including wildlife conservation, flood alleviation, clean water supplies and carbon sequestration. Also, encouragingly, there has been renewed interest in food from the wild, and traditional crafts involving our native timbers. There is no inherent reason why we could not use fruits and timber from our own local woods again, and we hope that the arboretum may help to stimulate this revival.

Judith Parry

Heartwood Arboretum

The Master Plan

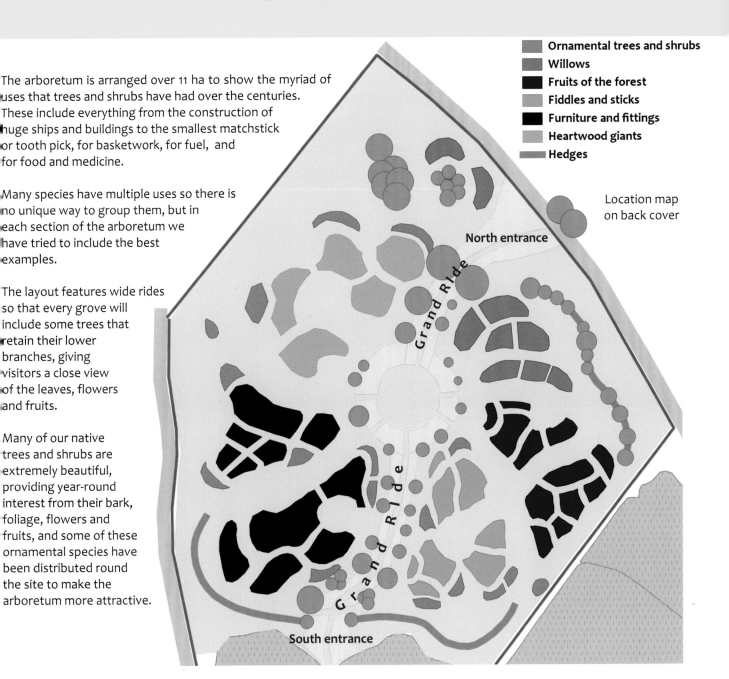

The arboretum is arranged over 11 ha to show the myriad of uses that trees and shrubs have had over the centuries. These include everything from the construction of huge ships and buildings to the smallest matchstick or tooth pick, for basketwork, for fuel, and for food and medicine.

Many species have multiple uses so there is no unique way to group them, but in each section of the arboretum we have tried to include the best examples.

The layout features wide rides so that every grove will include some trees that retain their lower branches, giving visitors a close view of the leaves, flowers and fruits.

Many of our native trees and shrubs are extremely beautiful, providing year-round interest from their bark, foliage, flowers and fruits, and some of these ornamental species have been distributed round the site to make the arboretum more attractive.

Legend:
- Ornamental trees and shrubs
- Willows
- Fruits of the forest
- Fiddles and sticks
- Furniture and fittings
- Heartwood giants
- Hedges

Location map on back cover

North entrance

Grand Ride

South entrance

The Grand Ride

Walking down the Grand Ride from the south entrance takes you through a swathe of native wild flowers and an avenue with individual specimens of most of the major tree species.

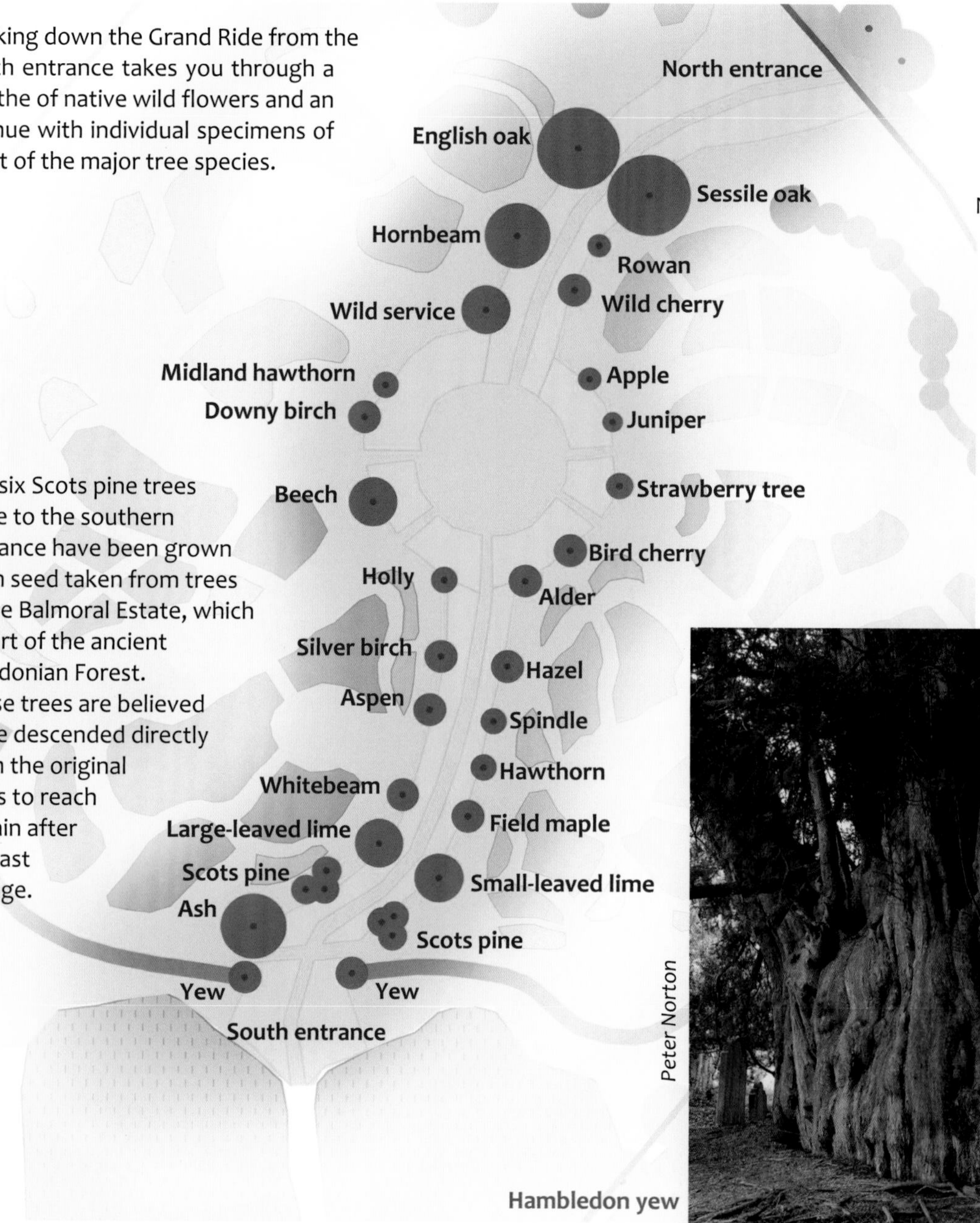

The six Scots pine trees close to the southern entrance have been grown from seed taken from trees in the Balmoral Estate, which is part of the ancient Caledonian Forest. These trees are believed to be descended directly from the original trees to reach Britain after the last ice-age.

Notice the two yew trees at the south entrance, which have been grown from cuttings taken from the "Hambledon Yew" in a churchyard in Surrey. It has a girth of 9.5 m and is believed to be a thousand years old. They were supplied by the Conservation Foundation.

North entrance

English oak

Sessile oak

Hornbeam

Rowan

Wild service

Wild cherry

Midland hawthorn

Apple

Downy birch

Juniper

Beech

Strawberry tree

Bird cherry

Holly

Alder

Silver birch

Hazel

Aspen

Spindle

Whitebeam

Hawthorn

Large-leaved lime

Field maple

Scots pine

Small-leaved lime

Ash

Scots pine

Yew

Yew

South entrance

Peter Norton

Hambledon yew

Hedges and woodland meadow

The most widespread use of trees and shrubs today is in hedges, which give our landscape its characteristic mosaic of fields. Almost any species of native tree and shrub may appear in a hedge, and here we have planted 450 m of what is perhaps the ultimate "species-rich" hedge with more than 40 species present. After a few years' growth the hedges will be layed in the South of England style with hazel stakes and binders.

The original purpose of laying a hedge was to thicken the bottom so that it is stock-proof. Layed hedges are also of huge environmental value producing cover and food for a wide variety of wild animals, birds and insects. By providing a link between woodland and other landscape features, hedgerows act as corridors for animals to use. Some of the hedge trees will be allowed to grow as standards to their full height, and others, such as white willow, crack willow and black poplar will be pollarded (regularly cut back to a height of 2-5 m).

Trees are also grown in meadows as individuals or small groups providing shelter for farm animals.

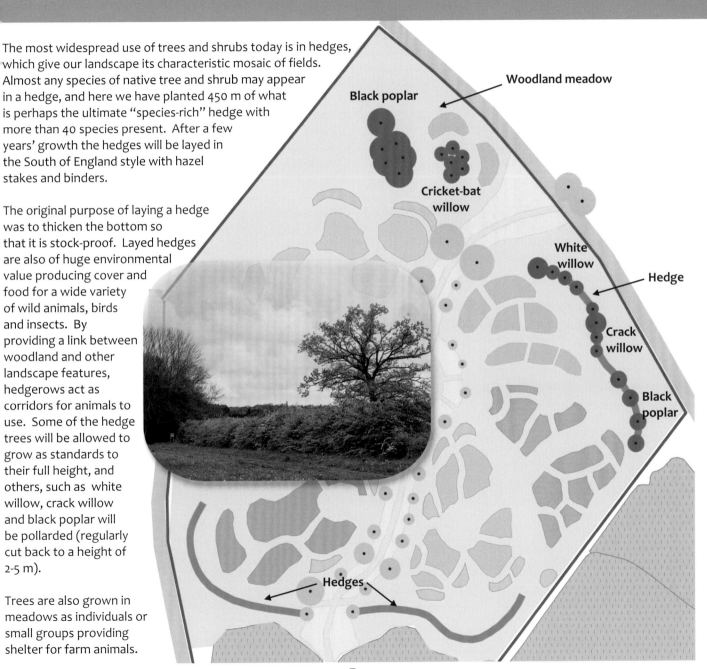

Woodland meadow

Black poplar

Cricket-bat willow

White willow

Hedge

Crack willow

Black poplar

Hedges

White willow
Salix alba

Cricket bat willow
Salix alba var. *caerulea*

Description

A tall (25 m) deciduous tree with grey-brown bark that develops deep fissures with age. Leaves are pale and slender with white downy undersides. Male and female catkins grow on separate trees.

Female catkins

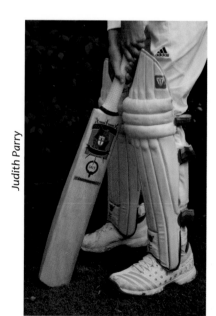

Judith Parry

Male catkin

Natural occurrence

Widespread throughout all of the British Isles except the Scottish Highlands. Widespread in Hertfordshire, especially near streams.

Properties and traditional uses

Its slender flexible stems are ideal for basketwork. When pollarded the young shoots were used as animal feed.

Description

A cultivated variety of white willow that is grown almost exclusively for making cricket bats.

Natural occurrence

It grows in plantations but seems not to occur naturally. Those in the River Ver valley between Redbourn and St. Albans are harvested regularly by J. S. Wright & Sons, cricket bat manufacturers.

Properties and traditional uses

It is coppiced (cut back to within 10 cm of the ground) when young and new shoots grow to a height of 3-4 m. These are cut off in the late winter and planted, and in subsequent years all the side shoots are removed from the stem to a height of 3 m so that the trunk is straight-grained and free from knots. After about 20 years the tree can be harvested and cricket bats made from the straight-grained trunk.

The "Agincourt"

A cricket bat made by J. S. Wright to celebrate 600 years since the battle in 1415

Crack willow
Salix fragilis

Description
A large (25 m) tree. Twigs and branches commonly fall off with a crack: hence the name. It is similar to white willow, though leaves are shorter and without silky white hairs on the underside.

Female catkins

Natural occurrence
Widespread throughout the British Isles except for the Scottish Highlands. Frequent in Hertfordshire: usually planted, but also occurring naturally along rivers and streams.

Properties and traditional uses
It has slender flexible stems, and along with other willows it has been used for basket making.

Black poplar
Populus nigra

Supplied by the Aylesbury Vale District Council from their black poplar clonal collection.

Description
A large (35 m) and very rare tree once planted along waterways and in hedgerows, and frequently pollarded. Most planted trees are male because the female trees make a mess producing a large amount of fluffy cotton-like seeds. Famously, they feature in "The Hay Wain" by Constable.

Natural occurrence
In a few isolated pockets including the Aylesbury Vale.

Properties and traditional uses
It has fine textured wood that resists shock and was used for carts, floorboards, clogs and artificial limbs.

Old black poplar pollards. Long Marston, Vale of Aylesbury.

Willows

Most of the willows here were provided by Rothamsted Research, Harpenden, from the National Willow Collection.
All willows are dioecious, with male and female catkins on separate plants.
We have both male and female plants in the arboretum.

There are no fewer than seven native willow species that grow into trees, and all are present in the arboretum. There are a further ten species that grow as shrubs, and we have the four that grow more than a metre tall. Two of the tree species are being grown in the hedge and are described in that section.

It is hard, now, to realise how important willows were for many centuries for basket making, and even during the Second World War there were 630 basket manufacturers in the UK employing 7,000 basket makers. Everything dropped by parachute was in a robust willow basket.

Willow is still planted alongside rivers to stabilise the banks. In earlier years they would often be pollarded, with the cuttings used as fodder for farm animals during a summer drought. For centuries it has been known that willow bark helps relieve pain. In 1829 it was discovered that the active ingredient was salicin, from which Aspirin was derived. It is thought that willows may also contain compounds that could be used to treat some forms of cancer.

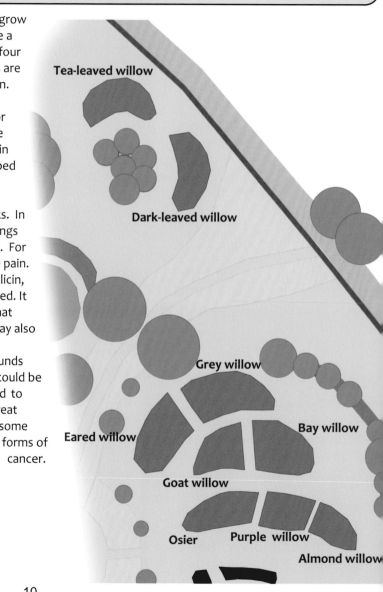

Tea-leaved willow

Dark-leaved willow

Grey willow

Bay willow

Eared willow

Goat willow

Osier

Purple willow

Almond willow

Goat willow
Salix caprea

Grey willow
Salix cinerea

Description
A medium sized deciduous tree (10 m) also known as pussy willow after the silky grey male catkins, which resemble a cat's paw and ripen to be covered with yellow pollen.

Description
A small deciduous tree (6-10 m) with broad leaves. It is sometimes known as common sallow and is closely related to goat willow with which it readily hybridises. It is also sometimes known as pussy willow. Its silky grey male catkins are similar to those of goat willow, but more slender.

Ruari Burnett

Male catkins

Female catkins

Female catkins release tiny seeds with white fluffy tufts.

Colin Legg

Goat willow and grey willow have broader leaves than most willows and are often referred to as sallows.

The leaves differ from those of goat willow in that the widest point is nearer to the tip than to the base.

Natural occurrence
Widespread across Britain and throughout Hertfordshire. Favours semi-natural woodland and old wooded hedgerows on damp soils, but also colonises disturbed sites.

Natural occurrence
It is widespread in woodlands and wetlands throughout eastern England including Hertfordshire where the subspecies *sp. oleifolia* is the most common.

Properties and traditional uses
The bark has been used for tanning leather, and the wood has been made into charcoal for gunpowder. It is valuable for biodiversity as many butterfly and moth larva feed on it including the purple emperor butterfly.

Properties and traditional uses
It may be grown on waste or derelict land, and hence it is useful for reclamation planting. Also used for stabilising wet soils and river banks. Like goat willow it is a valuable food plant for the purple emperor butterfly and several moth species.

Bay willow
Salix pentandra

Osier
Salix viminalis

Description
Medium sized tree (10 m) with leaves that look and smell like those of the bay tree. Male trees have showy catkins.

Description
Small (6 m), but very fast growing willow tree. Leaves are long and thin (20x1 cm).

Natural occurrence
Widespread throughout the British Isles, but not common in Hertfordshire.

WTML Vivien Wilson

Properties and traditional uses
Osier grows at a prodigious rate reaching over 2 m in its first year. In

Note: male and female catkins would not be on the same tree

the arboretum a few male and female trees are being allowed to grow to full size, but most will be coppiced on a 3-year rotation as they would be when grown for fuel.
It is also valuable for basket making, and is planted to clean up contaminated land.

Natural occurrence
Mainly found in northern England, southern Scotland and Northern Ireland. Widespread but rare in Hertfordshire; where it does occur it has always been introduced.

Properties and traditional uses
The bay willow's glossy leaves make it more decorative than many other willows, so it is often planted as an ornamental tree.

Osier sprouting after first year of coppicing

Purple willow
Salix purpurea

Description
Large (5 m) shrub with reddish purple stems and slender glossy green leaves with bluish underside.

Natural occurrence
Fairly widely distributed throughout the British Isles except in mountainous regions. In Hertfordshire there are a few plants by streams and in open scrub and hedgerows, though it is rare and decreasing.

Properties and traditional uses
Prized for gardens and by basket makers for its beautiful purple stems. Catkins crowd the stems in the spring giving it added interest as an ornamental plant. In the arboretum some shrubs will be allowed to grow to full size but most will be coppiced annually for local basket makers to use.

Almond willow
Salix triandra

Description
A medium sized tree (10 m). Leaves are glossy green, long and narrow, with regularly and conspicuously serrated edges and silvery undersides. It has long male catkins.

Male catkin

Natural occurrence
Widespread throughout south and east England. Rare in Hertfordshire, though a few occur in areas where it was probably grown for basket making.

Properties and traditional uses
Valuable for basket making. Some of our trees will be allowed to grow to full size but most will be coppiced annually for local basket makers to use.

Eared willow
Salix aurita

Tea-leaved willow
Salix phylicifolia

Dark-leaved willow
Salix myrsinifolia

Description

A large (3 m) multi-stemmed shrub in the sallow group. Its broad leaves have

ear-like stipules at the base.

Natural occurrence

Widespread throughout all of the British Isles except East Anglia. It is absent from Hertfordshire, except for a few isolated occurrences where shrubs have probably been introduced. It favours the acid ground of bogs and brooks.

Properties and traditional uses

It has been used to stabilise waste ground and slag heaps. It is an important part of damp ecosystems and provides food for many invertebrates.

Description

A large shrub (4 m). Twigs usually reddish-brown becoming dark in winter. Leaves are leathery, glossy green above and glaucous (bluish-grey) below, and resemble those of the tea plant. They lack the large stipules of the dark-leaved willow.

Natural occurrence

Officially classified as rare, and found only in northern England and Scotland. It grows by ponds, streams and rivers, and in damp rocky places, preferring neutral or alkaline soils. There are no current records in Hertfordshire.

Properties and traditional uses

No known uses, though it is available for gardens.

Description

A large shrub (4 m) or, less often, a small tree. Stems downy at first becoming smoother and dull brown or black with age. Leaves dark green above but glaucous below; toothed with large ear-like stipules at the base. It can readily be distinguished from other willows because damaged or bruised leaves rapidly turn black.

Natural occurrence

Found mainly in northern England and Scotland. It grows mainly on rocks or on gravelly river banks and lake shores, less frequently in thickets on marshy ground or by wet woodland margins. There are no current records in Hertfordshire.

Properties and traditional uses

It is available for gardens, and described by one nursery as "an absolutely gorgeous willow with a wonderfully pitch black bark, which in the sunshine has a purple sheen to it".

Fruits of the forest

Many of our trees and shrubs have fruits that would have been harvested traditionally to make a wide range of jams, jellies and alcoholic drinks, but nowadays most of the fruit we eat comes from cultivated varieties, and often from species not native to the British Isles. There are several fruit species, such as wild pear, bullace (plum) and damson, which are not native but used to be cultivated and have now become naturalised. These are not included in the arboretum

There are still a few companies that specialise in drinks and preserves made from the fruit of native trees and shrubs.

In addition to the trees and shrubs in this section there are others that have food value. For example bees make honey from the flowers of lime trees, hawthorn berries can be used to make a sauce, and acorns used to be fed to pigs.

Strawberry tree

Plymouth pear

Wild cherry

Juniper

Crab apple

Rowan

Bird cherry

Hazel

Sea buckthorn

Wild service

Elder

Blackthorn

Elderberry Wine '16

SLOE GIN

crab apple jelly

Plymouth pear
Pyrus cordata

Plymouth pear saplings are not readily available from commercial nurseries, but Kew is producing some for us from cuttings and from seeds from the Millennium Seed Bank, and they will be planted in autumn 2018.

Description
A small tree (8 m), with purplish twigs and leaves that vary

from elliptical to round with a wedge-shaped, rounded or heart-shaped base. The fruit has a long stem, and is small, hard, and round, with a woody appearance.

Nature Photographers Ltd/WTML

Natural occurrence
One of the rarest trees in the British Isles being found only in seven locations near to Plymouth, Devon, and Truro, Cornwall. The species is largely confined to western Europe, though it also occurs in North Africa and the Near East. It is not self-fertile, and sets none or very few seeds each year. It does, however, reproduce from suckers.

Properties and traditional uses
The fruits are not edible but it hybridises well with domestic pears, so may have potential value for breeding in the future. The fruit is eaten by birds.

Strawberry tree
Arbutus unedo

Description
An extremely beautiful small evergreen tree (8 m) with dark green leathery leaves and rough brown bark. The flowers are white and bell shaped and the strawberry-like fruit is red.

All photos by Alla Maschinova

Natural occurrence
It is found in southwest Ireland and at a few sites in southern England. It is a common tree in Mediterranean countries and is believed to be native in Ireland. It is not found in Hertfordshire except as a garden plant. It is a little susceptible to frost, but we hope ours will survive!

Properties and traditional uses
Used commonly as an ornamental tree in Britain, but used for jam, beverages and liqueurs in southern Europe.

Wild cherry
Prunus avium

Description
Mature trees can grow to 25 m and live for up to 60 years. The shiny bark is a

deep reddish-brown with prominent cream-coloured horizontal lines. Large toothed and pointed leaves are glossy and fade to orange and deep crimson in autumn. Flowers in clusters are followed by orange or red cherries.

Natural occurrence
Common through England and most of Ireland and Scotland, where it is known as gean. A common native tree in Hertfordshire, but also widely planted.

Properties and traditional uses
The second part of its botanical name, *avium*, refers to birds that eat the cherries and disperse the seed. The tree was valued for the fruit. The wood is hard and strong and is used for decorative veneers and furniture. There are many popular ornamental cultivars.

Bird cherry
Prunus padus

Description
A medium tree (15 m) with toothed, ovate leaves that are not glossy and turn yellow in autumn. Pendant racemes of fragrant white flowers, 1 cm wide, open in late spring and are followed by small, bitter black fruits.

Natural occurrence
Widespread, though less common in southern Ireland and south and southwest England. Very few records in Hertfordshire, and all thought to be introduced.

Properties and traditional uses
The tree is valuable for wildlife, producing nectar and pollen in the spring and fruit in the autumn. The bitter fruit is not palatable, though they can apparently be used to make a liqueur or to dye wool. The bark smells strongly and was said to ward off the plague.

Crab apple
Malus sylvestris

Juniper
Juniperus communis

Description

A small tree (9 m) with irregular, rounded shape, and with spiny branches becoming quite gnarled in old age. The flowers are sweetly scented. The fruit is small, green and extremely sour.

Natural occurrence

It grows all over England, though less in Scotland and Ireland. It is widespread in woods and hedgerows in Hertfordshire, though less common than escaped domestic apples.

Properties and traditional uses

Our thousands of cultivated apple varieties come primarily from a species native to the northern slopes of the Tien Shan mountain range that stretches from China to Uzbekistan, though there may well be some crab apple genes included. One theory is that bears living in that region favoured the sweetest apples and so spread the pips and helped the evolution of the sweet apples we now enjoy. Our native crab apple is used as a pollinator in commercial orchards and makes excellent crab apple jelly.

Description

A large (6 m), dioecious (with male and female flowers on separate plants), evergreen shrub. Small needle-like green leaves have broad silver bands on the inner side. Male bushes have small yellow flowers near the tips of twigs. Female trees have green flowers that are wind-pollinated and turn into purple, aromatic, berry-like cones.

Colin Legg

WTML Laurie Campbell

Natural occurrence

Widespread in Scotland, but patchy distribution in England and Wales and confined to the west and north coasts of Ireland. A rare plant in Hertfordshire, but occurs on both acid heath and chalk grassland. The nearest are probably those on the Mid-Herts golf course 3 miles north of the arboretum.

Properties and traditional uses

The most famous use for the berries is as a flavouring for gin, but they were also a popular ingredient in liqueurs and sauces.

Rowan
Sorbus aucuparia

Description
An attractive, medium sized tree (15 m) with silvery grey bark and hairy, purple leaf buds. Leaves are pinnate with 5-8 pairs of leaflets and one terminal leaflet. Creamy white flowers are in dense clusters and are followed by red berries.

Colin Legg

Natural occurrence
Common across the whole of the British Isles. In Hertfordshire it used to be restricted to the southwest, but now widespread as cultivated trees have escaped.

Properties and traditional uses
Wood is hard and tough, but not particularly durable. It is sometimes used for turning, furniture, craftwork and engraving. Rowan berries are edible for humans. They are sour, but rich in vitamin C, and can be used to make a jelly to accompany meats.

Wild service
Sorbus torminalis

Description
A rare medium sized tree (20 m) related to rowan and whitebeam. The lobed leaves turn a rich, coppery red in autumn. The green-brown oval fruits are 10–15 mm diameter and patterned with small pale spots when mature.

Natural occurrence
A native of Wales and central and southern England preferring clay and neutral and slightly acid soils. Frequent but patchy in the south of Hertfordshire, but rare in the north.

Properties and traditional uses
The wood has a fine grain and silvery sheen, though it has never been widely used. The fruits, known as chequers, can be used to flavour alcoholic drinks such as beer and whisky, and it is thought that pubs called "The Chequers" are named after them.

Sea buckthorn
Hippophae rhamnoides

Hazel
Corylus avellana

Description

A large shrub (7 m) with thorny shoots and narrow, willow-like silvery leaves. Flowers are small and yellow, but on female plants they are often followed by a heavy crop of small bright orange berries.

Colin Legg

Natural occurrence

Widespread along almost all the coasts of the British Isles. Does not belong in Hertfordshire, though occasional plants have been found.

Properties and traditional uses

Sea buckthorn has been planted to stabilise sand dunes, but sometimes becomes invasive and shades out other species. The leaves and berries are both edible, and the berries can be made into jam, fruit concentrate or oil. Sea buckthorn oil is available as a food supplement and it is said that Genghis Khan used it to keep his soldiers strong and active!

Description

Hazel will grow into a small tree (5-10 m). Leaves are round to oval, doubly toothed, hairy and pointed at the tip. They turn yellow before falling in autumn. Bright yellow male catkins appear in February. After pollination the small, bright red female flowers produce nuts with a woody shell surrounded by a cup of leafy bracts.

Colin Legg

WTML Richard Becker

Colin Legg

Red female catkin

Natural occurrence

Common right across the British Isles. Ubiquitous in Hertfordshire where much of it would have been coppiced, as described in the next section.

Properties and traditional uses

Hazel was grown in the UK for large-scale nut production until the early 1900s. Cultivated varieties (known as cob-nuts) are still grown in Kent, but most of our hazelnuts are now imported.

WTML Ben Lee

Elder
Sambucus nigra

Description
Elder is a small deciduous tree (6 m, though occasionally as tall as 15 m). It has a grey-brown corky bark and pinnate leaves with five to seven toothed leaflets.

Ruari Burnett

Flowers are borne on large flat heads, 10-30 cm across, and are creamy white and highly scented. The flowers develop into small, purple-black, sour berries, which ripen from late summer to autumn.

WTML Ben Lee

Natural occurrence
Common and very widespread throughout the British Isles and in the woods, hedges and scrub areas of Hertfordshire.

Properties and traditional uses
Both flowers and berries can be made into excellent wines, and sparkling white wine can be made from the flowers. The berries also provide food for birds.

Blackthorn
Prunus spinosa

Description
Blackthorn is a small deciduous tree (5 m). It is densely branched and has vicious thorns. It is one of the first trees to flower in the spring, often as early as February, and is covered with masses of small white flowers before the small narrow leaves unfold. The bark is very dark, almost black, and the fruits, known as sloes, are blue-black and 10 mm across.

Linda McArdell

Natural occurrence
Common and very widespread occurring in all but the Highlands and Flow Country of Scotland, and some of the Scottish islands. Also common throughout Hertfordshire, though can be confused with wild plum, which is not a native species.

Properties and traditional uses
Famously used for making sloe gin, but the sloes can also be used to make wine and preserves. The wood is hardwearing and tough and was traditionally used for making walking sticks and tool parts.

Blackthorn is invaluable for wildlife, providing nectar in the spring, leaves that provide food for the caterpillars of many moth and butterfly species, and dense foliage that is ideal for birds' nests.

Fiddles and sticks

It is wood that defines trees and shrubs, and each species has wood with a unique structure and with different mechanical and aesthetic properties. Over the centuries it was found that for every application some species of trees out-perform all others, for example, by having durability against rot and woodworm or having a close grain that polishes well.

So whether you wish to make a violin or a walking stick, start by selecting wood from the right tree! But remember that quality is equally affected by soil conditions, degree of exposure and the contrast between cold and warm climates.

In this section you will find species that have been used for making violins and walking sticks, and also those that are ideal for underwater foundations, for engraving, for sculpture, and for toothpicks and spindles.

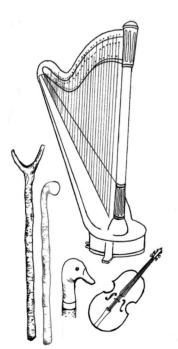

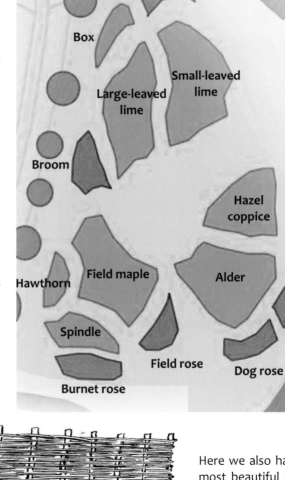

Wayfaring tree

Box

Small-leaved lime

Large-leaved lime

Broom

Hazel coppice

Sweet briar

Hawthorn

Field maple

Alder

Broom

Spindle

Field rose

Dog rose

Burnet rose

Here we also have some of the most beautiful of our shrubs including broom and four of the twelve native roses.

Small-leaved lime
Tilia cordata

Large-leaved lime
Tilia platyphyllos

Description
Small-leaved lime is a large (25 m) deciduous tree. Leaves are 3-8 cm in length, heart shaped, and with a pointed tip.

Flowers hang in clusters of 4 to 10 and are followed by smooth oval fruits with pointed tips. The small-leaved lime often suckers from the base. A coppiced small-leaved lime at Westonbirt is probably about 2000 years old, making it one of the oldest tree in the UK.

Natural occurrence
It used to be one of our dominant woodland trees, but numbers have declined and its presence is now often regarded as an indicator of an ancient wood. It occurs throughout most of England, though rare or absent from the southwest, and in Scotland and Ireland. No longer occurs in Hertfordshire as a wild tree, but is used in amenity plantings.

Our trees were supplied by The Community Tree Trust and were grown from seeds sourced in Barton, Bedfordshire.

Description
The large-leaved lime is one of our largest native trees growing to a massive 30 m. Leaves are 6-12 cm long, heart shaped, and with a pointed tip. They are softly furry and have hairy stalks. Flowers are green-yellow and hang in clusters of two to five, followed by small round fruits with a pointed tip.

WTML Deborah Carvill

Natural occurrence
Large-leaved limes are widespread, but not common, across England, Wales and southern Scotland. In Hertfordshire, there are thought to be only a few wild trees, though planted specimens are fairly common.

Properties and traditional uses
Lime wood is light coloured, soft, easily worked, and was known to the Romans as 'the tree of a thousand uses'. It has been used to make cups, ladles, bowls, toys, dug-out canoes, beehive frames and Morris dancing sticks. It also has the right properties for a piano sounding board, though spruce is now more commonly used. The flowers are attractive to bees and make excellent honey. They can also be used to make tea, sold as a health drink.

In addition to the large-leaved and small-leaved limes there is also the "Common" lime, which is a hybrid between the two species. The surest way to distinguish the three limes is from the underside of the leaf, where small-leaved lime has tufts of reddish-brown hairs at the vein junctions; common lime has tufts of white hairs, and the large-leaved lime has hairs all over.

Small-leaved lime

Common lime

Large-leaved lime

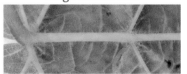

Box
Buxus sempervirens

Hazel coppice
Corylus avellana

Description

Common box is a small (5 m), slow-growing evergreen tree, though it can occasionally grow to 12 m. It has a compact habit, with smooth grey bark which fissures with age, and green, downy stems. Leaves are small (10x25 mm), shiny, leathery and dark green. Male and female flowers are clustered together and are small and green-yellow. The fruit, when ripe, have a brown, woody seed case.

Natural occurrence

Box is widespread throughout England and southern Scotland, but rare or non-existent elsewhere. In Hertfordshire it is rare, and probably exists only where it has been planted.

Properties and traditional uses

Box produces the densest native wood, and sinks in water. It is very hard and fine grained, so has been used for engraving where its durability proved able to stand up to many thousands of impressions without deteriorating. It has also been used for violin pegs, and parts of other musical instruments. It is commonly used for ornamental hedges and topiary.

Engraving on box wood by Chris Daunt

Description

The hazel tree, which was described in the previous section, can be grown as a coppice by cutting all the shoots (known as poles) back to within about 10 cm of the ground every 5 to 10 years. Many old coppices are no longer cut and have become overgrown.

Natural occurrence

Hazel was coppiced in all parts of the British Isles, though there are now many more old coppices in the south of England than elsewhere. In Hertfordshire it was commonly grown with scattered standard trees of ash, field maple, oak or hornbeam.

Properties and traditional uses

The shoots are supple, readily split, and can be easily twisted and woven by hand. Traditionally they have been used to make a range of products, including: wattles ('wattle and daub' plaster), sheep hurdles, sheep cages (to hold fodder), barrel hoops (for dry or solid goods), garden fencing, walking sticks, pea and bean sticks, thatching spars, hedge stakes and binders, faggots (fuel for kilns and ovens), and fascines (bundles of rods for river control or revetments). At Heartwood we have layed many hedges and used our own hazel poles for the stakes and binders.

24

Hawthorn
Crataegus monogyna

Field maple
Acer campestre

Description

Hawthorn is a medium sized tree (10-15 m) and is covered with thorns. The leaves are about 6 cm long and are lobed and toothed. It flowers in the early spring producing masses of

Linda McArdell

white, highly scented blossom, also known as May blossom. It possibly gives its name to the saying "Ne'er cast a clout till May be out". Berries, or haws, are bright red.

Natural occurrence

Hawthorn can be found in every part of the British Isles. It occurs everywhere in the hedgerows and woods of Hertfordshire. Many have been planted recently, though plantings include non-native hawthorn species.

Properties and traditional uses

Hawthorn is a favourite species for hedges as it is easy to lay producing a tough, spiny, stock-proof barrier. The wood is very hard and fine-grained making it good for turning, engraving and for mallet heads, tool handles, boxes, boat parts. It also makes an attractive veneer.

The haws are eaten greedily by thrushes in the winter but can also can be used to make wines and preserves. Hugh Fearnley-Whittingstall gives a recipe for haw-sin sauce - 'really good', he says.

Description

Field maple is a small tree (8 m), though very old trees may grow to double this height. Leaves are small with five lobes, and they fade to a rich golden yellow in the autumn.

WTML Ben Lee

Flowers are small, but the winged seeds are large and dispersed by the wind. It should not be confused with the sycamore, which was probably introduced to Britain in the Middle Ages.

Natural occurrence

Field Maple is found throughout England, Wales and southern Scotland, but is less common in the north of Scotland and in Ireland. It is abundant in the woods and hedgerows of Hertfordshire, and thrives on many soil types.

Properties and traditional uses

Field maple produces the hardest, highest density timber of all European maples. It is a warm creamy-brown colour with a silky sheen. Traditional uses included dance floors, wood-turning, carving and making musical instruments, particularly violins and harps. The wood polishes well and can be used as a veneer.

This gorgeous rosewood guitar was made by Kevin Aram of Aram Guitars, who uses maple, black dyed maple, pear, yew and spalted beech. Some woods are chosen for their acoustic or structural properties, others for ornamentation.

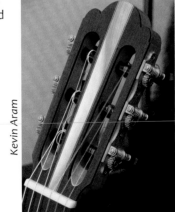

Kevin Aram

Alder
Alnus glutinosa

Description

Alder is a large (25 m) tree with a dark fissured bark. Twigs have a light brown spotted stem which turns red towards the top, and young twigs are sticky. Leaf buds are purple or grey,

Alla Maschinova

and the 3-9 cm dark green leaves are racquet-shaped and leathery with serrated edges. Between February and April the trees are covered with male catkins (purple turning to yellow) and female catkins (red turning to green), followed by small cone-like fruits in the winter. Alder and sea buckthorn are unique among our native trees and shrubs in having root nodules with bacteria that fix nitrogen.

Colin Legg

Natural occurrence

Alder grows in all parts of the British Isles. It is widespread in Hertfordshire, especially beside rivers and in wet areas.

Properties and traditional uses

Alder wood is soft, but extremely durable when totally immersed in water. Much of Venice is built on alder piles, and it has been used to strengthen river banks, where some posts will take root and grow giving additional stability. It is used for sluices and small boats. Alder also makes the best charcoal for gunpowder. Formerly alder was used for tanning and as a source of dyes for wool and linen. It is now planted on poor and water-logged soils to improve fertility. The seeds are loved by goldfinches, siskins and redpolls.

Spindle
Euonymous europaeus

Description

Spindle is a large (3 m) and beautiful shrub, though can grow much larger in favourable conditions. The bark and twigs are deep green, becoming darker with age, and have light brown, corky markings. Twigs are thin and straight. Leaves are shiny and slightly waxy, and have tiny sharp teeth along the edges. They turn a rich orange-red before falling in autumn. The insect pollinated flowers have four petals and grow in clusters. It is stunningly beautiful in the autumn with bright pink four-lobed fruits with orange seeds.

Natural occurrence

Spindle may be found in all parts of England, Wales and Ireland, but only in the southeast of Scotland. In Hertfordshire it is a characteristic shrub of hedgerows, especially on the clay soils in the east and west of the county.

WTML

Properties and traditional uses

Spindle timber is creamy white, hard and dense. In the past it was used to make 'spindles' for spinning and holding wool (hence its name), as well as skewers, toothpicks, pegs and knitting needles. It is now used to make high quality charcoal for artists, and cultivated forms are grown in gardens for their berries and autumn colour.

Ornamental shrubs in this section

Wayfaring tree
Viburnum lantana

Broom
Cytisus scoparius

Description

The wayfaring tree is a large (5 m) shrub with large, oval, slightly wrinkly leaves with round toothed edges. Leaves are opposite one another on the twigs, and the undersides are densely covered with soft grey hairs. Lots of small identical five-petalled cream flowers form together in large flat-topped heads. The fruits start red and turn black. They are poisonous.

Natural occurrence

The wayfaring-tree may be found throughout central and southern England and most of Wales, but is uncommon or absent elsewhere.
It is a characteristic shrub of old hedgerows in Hertfordshire, especially in the north and west, but also occurs elsewhere wherever chalk comes to the surface.

Properties and traditional uses

It is often planted as an ornamental shrub. It provides food for many birds and insects.

Description

Broom is a medium (1.5 m), short-lived, evergreen shrub with small leaves with three leaflets. In spring and early summer it produces a

dazzling display with masses of bright yellow pea-like flowers. These are followed by pods of seeds.

Natural occurrence

Broom occurs in all parts of the British Isles. In Hertfordshire it occurs, but is uncommon, in central and southeast regions, preferring acidic sandy or gravelly soils.

Properties and traditional uses

Broom has been used to make green dyes from the leaves and stems, and yellow and brown dyes from the bark. It is a bitter narcotic herb and as with most of our native shrubs it has had medical value attributed to it. Its main use, however, is as an ornamental plant, with some variants having red central petals.

Burnet rose
Rosa spinosissima

Description
The burnet rose, also known as the Scotch rose, is a small (1 m) creeping shrub with numerous bristles and spines. Leaves have up to a dozen small leaflets. The young stems and prickles and the mature leaves tend to be red with young growth a bright scarlet, and older growth a deep maroon. The flowers are cream-white, although rarely also pale pink. They are 2-4 cm diameter with five petals, and produce distinctive globular dark purple to black hips.

Colin Legg

Natural occurrence
Widespread throughout coastal regions of the British Isles. One or two plants have been found in Hertfordshire, but all are likely to be planted or garden escapes.

Properties and traditional uses
The hips are rich in vitamins and minerals, and can, apparently, be made into a pleasant tasting fruity-flavoured tea. It is widely available as an ornamental rose, and has been used in breeding several garden hybrids.

Field rose
Rosa arvensis

Description
The field rose is a small (2 m) trailing shrub with numerous spines. Leaves have, typically, five to seven-toothed leaflets. Its fragrant flowers are white, and have a very conspicuous central mound of golden stamens. The hips are small and red.

Trailing stems

Natural occurrence
The field rose is common throughout central and southern England, Wales and eastern Ireland, and most plentiful in the hedgerows of the south of England. In Hertfordshire it is a frequent rose of old hedgerows, woodlands and wood margins. It is not found in more recent habitats.

Properties and traditional uses
The field rose enhances hedgerows as its arching branches are covered with white flowers. In gardens it is valued for its scent, and it can be used to make perfumes. It has been used in breeding several garden roses.

The field rose is the musk rose In Shakespeare's Midsummer Night's Dream, where Titania sleeps on a bank "With sweet musk roses and with eglantine".

Dog rose
Rosa canina

Sweet briar
Rosa rubiginosa

Description

The dog rose provides one of the most beautiful signs of approaching summer as its slightly scented white and pink flowers begin to open. In autumn bright red hips can be seen as flashes of colour among the leafless stems. It is a large (4 m) thorny climber with large curved spines. Leaves have 5 to 7 smaller leaflets. Leaf buds

are often affected by a gall known as robin's pin-cushion. They are caused by a gall wasp and look like a ball of fibrous red threads.

Natural occurrence

The dog rose is common throughout all of England, southern Scotland, and a few areas in the northeast and southwest of Ireland. It is widespread throughout the hedgerows, scrub, woodland and waste areas of Hertfordshire.

Properties and traditional uses

Rose hips are high in vitamin C and were traditionally used to make rose hip syrup. The hairs inside the hips are an irritant extracted to make an itching powder. It is widely available for horticultural use, but would be an uncomfortable plant in a small garden! Alba roses are an ancient group of roses that originated from a cross between the *Rosa canina* and the french rose, *Rosa gallica.* David Austin considers them to be among the most beautiful of the Old Roses.

Description

Sweet briar is a vigorous, medium sized (2.5 m) arching deciduous shrub with prickly stems bearing apple-scented foliage, and cupped single light pink flowers in summer, followed by ovoid red fruits.

Natural occurrence

There are records of sweet briar scattered across the whole of the British Isles, but they are plentiful only in southern England and Wales, and southeast Scotland. There have been only a handful of records in Hertfordshire, mostly, but not all, on chalk.

Properties and traditional uses

The sweet brier is referred to as 'eglantine' by Shakespeare. In addition to its pink flowers, it is valued for its scent, and for the red hips that form after the flowers and persist well into the winter. It is a parent of many garden hybrids. Tea can be made from the hips and it is considered a healthy way for people to get their daily dose of vitamin C and other nutrients. It is said that a cup of rose hip tea will provide the minimum daily adult dose of vitamin C, and that the British relied on rose hips and hops as the source of vitamins A and C during the second world war.

The wood from almost all of our trees can be used in furniture making, and will be valued for its strength or beauty. In this section of the arboretum we have some of those that are most widely used. The diversity of colour, grain and technical qualities of wood from our trees is extraordinary. In our native woodlands species were selected and managed to provide a huge range of vital and diverse timber products of the right quality for kilned boards, air-dried timber, green wood for structural frames and a myriad of other products.

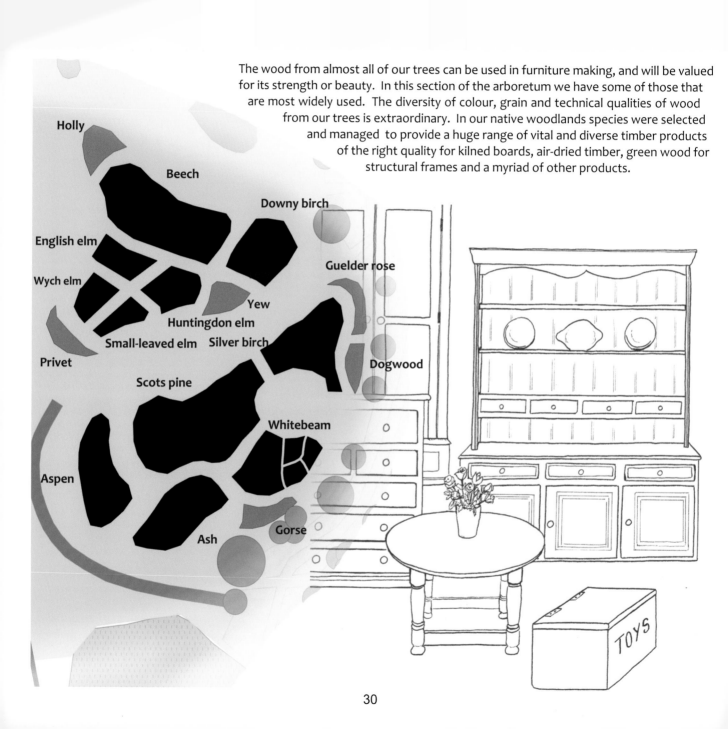

Holly

Beech

Downy birch

English elm

Wych elm

Guelder rose

Yew

Huntingdon elm

Small-leaved elm   Silver birch

Privet

Dogwood

Scots pine

Whitebeam

Aspen

Ash   Gorse

TOYS

Description

Beech is one of our largest (25 m) and loveliest trees, giving a stunning autumn display of yellows and oranges. It is often

Colin Legg

considered to be the queen of British trees. The bark is smooth, thin and grey. Young leaves (4-6 cm long) are lime green with silky hairs, and become darker green and hairless as they

WTML Ben Lee

mature. Nuts, known as beechmast, are in a hard, rough, woody shell.

Natural occurrence

Beech grows in all parts of the British Isles, but is native only in southern England. It is thought likely to suffer in the southeast of England if the climate becomes warmer and drier. Beech is native as a major component of the Chiltern woodlands in the west of Hertfordshire. It is also widespread in the centre and east of the county, but usually as planted trees.

Properties and traditional uses

Beech wood is used for making chairs, cabinets and cupboards. The nuts are edible, but were also once used to feed pigs. They can, apparently be roasted and used as a coffee substitute. Beech makes an excellent hedge with the advantage that when clipped it is slow to lose its leaves and provides a year-round screen.

Description

Scots pine is a large (30 m) evergreen conifer. It can be recognised easily by the orange bark on the upper trunk and branches. The needles are 2-6 cm long and grouped in pairs growing from a basal sheath. Male flowers release clouds of yellow pollen; female flowers produce small cones that mature to 3-8 cm long in their second year.

Natural occurrence

After the last ice-age Scots pine spread into England but then died out as the climate warmed. Other trees spread into Scotland from the landmass that was then to the west, and those have survived as the native Caledonian forest. Most trees in England, Wales and Ireland are of imported origin.

Properties and traditional uses

WTML Geoff Hall

The wood of Scots pine is one of the strongest softwoods available and is widely used in the construction industry and in joinery. It is also used for telegraph poles, pit props and fencing.

In 2014 the Scots pine was voted overwhelmingly to be Scotland's favourite tree.

There has been some confusion over the naming of English elms as many trees that were considered to be independent species are now regarded as varieties of the three major species included in the arboretum. For example the Plots elm, listed by the Royal Horticultural Society, is now believed to be a variety of the small-leaved elm, *Ulmus minor*. There are also many hybrids, of which we include only the Huntingdon elm.

Elms, which propagate mainly from suckers and lack genetic diversity, were almost completely wiped out as trees by Dutch elm disease in the 1970s. Many thrive in hedgerows, though any that grow above a height of about 5 metres attract the beetle that spreads the Dutch elm fungus. All the elms in the arboretum have been supplied by the Conservation Foundation. They have been grown from cuttings taken from elm trees in England that have survived Dutch elm disease, and it is hoped that they will have genetic resistance. Time will tell!

Properties and traditional uses

Most sources of information on the uses of elm make no distinction between the different species. Elm wood is strong and durable with a tight-twisted grain, and is resistant to water. It has been used in decorative turning, and to make boats and boat parts, furniture, wheel hubs, wooden water pipes, floorboards and coffins. Many English towns, including Bristol, Reading, Exeter, Southampton, Hull and Liverpool, had water mains supplied from pipes made from elm wood, before metal pipes became available.

English elm is unusual in that even isolated trees grow straight and tall providing good wood for construction. Elm and oak were the woods of choice for barns in Hertfordshire, and elm has been used by Robert Somerville who built this beautiful barn near Welwyn.

Description

This large (40 m) tree, is thought by some to be a cloned variety of the small-leaved elm, and some think it may have been imported by the Romans for training vines, in which case it is not truly native. Elms in general can be identified by the asymmetric leaf base and double-toothed edge. Leaves of English elm are 5-9 cm long, almost circular in shape and rough on the upper surface. Leaf stalks and shoots are hairy. Trees often have suckers at their base.

Natural occurrence

Once an iconic tree of England, Wales and Ireland, it was almost completely wiped out as a tree by Dutch elm disease. It persists as a shrub in the hedgerows of Hertfordshire except the east where it is replaced by the small-leaved elm.

Description

The small-leaved elm is a large tree (30 m) but does not grow as tall as the English elm with which it is easily confused. The bark is grey-brown, often with crossing ridges. The twigs are brown and occasionally have corky 'wings' or ridges. Leaves are glossy, flat, 6-15 cm in length and double toothed. The leaves are smooth but leathery to the touch and this species is sometimes referred to as the smooth-leaved elm.

Natural occurrence

Once common in south and southeast England where almost all the mature trees have been wiped out by Dutch elm disease. It survives as a shrub and in hedgerows. The range of small-leaved elm in Hertfordshire overlaps with that of the English elm, but it is the dominant species in the east.

Description

Wych elm is very similar to English elm, though with larger (7-16 cm) leaves sporting one and sometimes three sharp points at the top. Flowers appear before the leaves in early spring. They are red-purple in colour and appear in clusters of 10 to 20

Photo from old wych elm coppice

Colin Legg

spaced out along the twigs and small branches. In winter twigs and buds are covered in orange hairs.

Natural occurrence

Once common across the whole of the British Isles, it has largely succumbed to Dutch Elm disease. It usually grows in hilly or rocky woodlands, or beside streams and ditches. It is hardier than the English elm so is found much further north and west and in parts of Scotland. In Hertfordshire it is a widespread component of semi-natural woodland, especially with beech or with ash/maple, and also occurs widely in ancient hedgerows.

Description

Huntingdon elm, sometimes called the Chichester elm, is a fast-growing and large (35 m) tree and is a cross between small-leaved elm and wych elm. It was raised from a seed in Huntingdon in 1760, though it probably also exists as a natural hybrid. It is included in the arboretum because it is thought the most likely of the elms to be resistant to Dutch elm disease. It has leaves up to 12x8 cm and is very similar to wych elm, with which it is easily confused.

Natural occurrence

Most of the Huntingdon elms are in central and eastern England, and have been planted. It has been recorded at many places in Hertfordshire.

Description

Silver birch is a large (25 m) and elegant tree with its striking white bark. As the tree matures the bark develops dark, diamond-shaped fissures. Leaves are light green, small and

triangular-shaped with a double-toothed edge (small teeth on the larger ones), and fade to yellow in autumn. Male and female catkins are found on the same tree, from April to May. Male catkins are long and yellow-brown in colour and pendant, female catkins are smaller, short, bright green and erect. Masses of tiny seeds are formed and spread far and wide by the wind. Birch grows rapidly, but rarely lives beyond 80 years.

Natural occurrence

Silver birch is common across the whole of England, Wales and Scotland, and also found in most parts of Ireland. It is found throughout Hertfordshire except in the north east.

Properties and traditional uses

Birch produces tough, heavy timber and is commonly used as the surface veneer on plywood. It has also been used to make furniture, parquet floor blocks, kitchen utensils and skis. In bygone years it was used to make the bobbins, spools and reels in the cotton industry. Silver birch provides food and habitat for more than 300 insect species, nesting holes for woodpeckers and seeds for the smaller finches to eat.

Description

Downy birch is very similar to silver birch, though typically slightly smaller (20 m). It can be distinguished by being somewhat more upright, and with bark that is more brown and with more obvious horizontal grooves. It also lacks the papery quality of the bark of silver birch. Leaves are single-toothed and triangular, but more rounded at the base than silver birch leaves. Leaf stalks are downy.

Colin Legg

Natural occurrence

Downy birch grows in all parts of the British Isles, and favours damp or even waterlogged conditions. It is found in many parts of Hertfordshire, but in many places there are also hybrids with silver birch.

Properties and traditional uses

In addition to the uses listed for silver birch both species have also been used, primarily in other countries, to provide canoe skins, and as a source of a brown dye. It is also possible to tap the trees to provide a rich sugary syrup or a variety of alcoholic drinks.

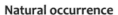

Description

Aspen is a beautiful tree growing to 20 m tall and with leaves that flutter, or shimmer in the slightest breeze. It suckers freely producing a dense thicket, and in the arboretum we have left a 10 m wide path all round to try to stop it invading other species. The bark is grey and often pitted with

diamond-shaped pores. Leaves are round with a flattened stem. When young they are coppery coloured, and in the autumn they turn a

vibrant yellow, or occasionally red. Aspen, in common with other poplar and willow species, is dioecious, having male and female catkins on different plants.

Natural occurrence

Aspen grows in all parts of the British Isles, though is not quite so common in Ireland. In Hertfordshire aspen is characteristic of acidic clay soils, mainly in the south and central areas.

Suckers growing away from main trunk

Properties and traditional uses

As a light weight wood it has been used to make oars, paddles and splints. It is also the best wood for lining saunas and steam baths.

Ash is currently being attacked by ash die-back, a fungal disease that arrived from continental Europe in about 2012. It is not known how many of our mature ash trees will succumb, but it is expected that a few will be resistant and will slowly replace those that die. We will plant ash when resistant strains are available.

Description

Ash trees can grow to a magnificent 30 m tall and live to the grand old age of 400 years. They are easily identified in the

winter by twigs that are smooth with distinctive black, velvety leaf buds. The composite leaves typically comprise 3 to 6 opposite pairs of light green oval leaflets with long

Donato Cinicolo

Seeds

Male flowers

tips. The winged seeds ripen in the spring and are dispersed by the wind. Surprisingly, ash and wild privet are both members of the olive family.

Natural occurrence

Ash may be found in all parts of the British Isles and is our third commonest tree. It is abundant in Hertfordshire. It grows readily and rapidly from seed and so colonises any bare soil within a hundred metres or so of a mature tree.

Properties and traditional uses

Ash wood is exceedingly tough and absorbs shocks without splintering, so it is widely used for spade, hammer and axe handles, and in sports equipment including snooker cues, oars, paddles and cricket stumps. Ash is the best wood for burning and can be burned when green.

Apomixis

The "*Sorbus*" family includes whitebeam, rowan, and wild service as British natives. It is unusual in that there are occasional crosses between these three species, and the progeny are apomictic – meaning that the seeds grow without being pollinated. All new progeny are, therefore, genetically identical to their parent tree and form a new 'species', though some would call them only a microspecies. Occasionally these new species cross again with one of the three original species and form yet more 'species'. *Sorbus* are the only native trees to be apomictic, though bramble and dandelion are also.

All of the apomictic whitebeams are very rare and are often confined to a specific location, for example the Isle of Arran, or Cheddar Gorge. Many thrive in steep rocky coastal areas where other trees would struggle to survive.

The Royal Horticultural Society lists no less than 17 of these very rare whitebeams, though others list many more. They fall into three groups according to parentage and leaf shape, and the four whitebeams in the arboretum include members of each group. They are arranged in the whitebeam area as shown below.

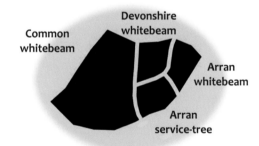

Properties and traditional uses

Whitebeam timber is fine-grained, hard and white. Traditional uses included wood-turning and fine joinery, including chairs, beams, cogs and wheels in machinery, though it is now rarely available and little used. The berries are said to be edible when nearly rotten! The whitebeam is prized for its beautiful foliage and colourful berries and is commonly planted as a medium sized ornamental tree.

Description

Common whitebeam is a compact, medium height (20 m) tree with smooth grey bark and twigs, and brick red shoots. Leaves are thick, oval and irregularly toothed, with the underneath covered in white, felt-like hair. When the leaves first unfold they look like magnolia flowers. They fade to a rich russet colour before falling in autumn. White flowers appear in clusters in May, and are followed by scarlet berries.

Natural occurrence

Common whitebeam is native to southern England, but also occurs in most parts of England, Wales and Scotland. It is almost completely absent from Ireland. It occurs as a native tree in west Hertfordshire. It has frequently been planted as an ornamental tree, though some of these are a very similar European species.

Devon whitebeam
Sorbus devoniensis

Arran whitebeam
Sorbus arranensis

Arran service-tree
Sorbus pseudofennica

There are eight apomictic *Sorbus* species in Devon, including one that was originally known simply as the "No Parking Tree" after the road sign nailed to it! The Devon whitebeam is one of these, and we have several that were generously donated by Paignton Zoo, which has a conservation programme.

Both of these whitebeams are native to the Isle of Arran. They were purchased from Arran Trees, a nursery on the island.

Description

The Devon whitebeam (13 m) is probably a hybrid between common whitebeam and wild service, so has leaves that are generally oval with  shallow triangular lobes. White flowers are followed by orange berries.

Tracey Hamston

Natural occurrence

Devon whitebeam occur in small numbers only in Devon and a small area of southeast Ireland.

Description

The Arran whitebeam (8 m) is a complex hybrid involving the common whitebeam, rock whitebeam and rowan. The leaf shape is generally  oval, but with deep lobes.

Arran Trees

In other respects the tree is similar to the common whitebeam.

Natural occurrence

The Arran whitebeam is native to the Isle of Arran, though there are also a few trees on the mainland in Ayrshire. It is among the rarest trees in the world, with only 707 records in the National Biodiversity Network (NBN) dataset. They have survived as a species because they are tolerant of very harsh conditions at high altitude.

Description

The Arran service-tree (7 m) resulted from a further cross between the Arran whitebeam and rowan. It is sometimes known as the "bastard mountain ash" or, perhaps more accurately, as the "cut-leaved whitebeam". This further hybridisation results in leaves with even deeper indentations between the lobes, and the first lobe is often separated from the rest of the leaf. The flower is very similar to that of the Arran whitebeam, but larger.

Natural occurrence

The Arran service-tree is found only on the Isle of Arran, and is one of the rarest trees in Scotland. There are only 575 records in the NBN dataset.

Holly
Ilex aquifolium

Privet
Ligustrum vulgare

Description

Holly is one of our few large evergreen trees, the others being Scots pine and yew. It grows to a height of 25 m and produces a mass of prickly, dark green leaves. It is dioecious with four-petalled white flowers on both male and female trees, but the bright red berries on female trees in the autumn are far more conspicuous.

Ruari Burnett

Colin Legg

Natural occurrence

Holly grows all over the British Isles, with the possible exception of the extreme northeast of Scotland. It is found throughout Hertfordshire except on the clay and chalk in the north. It grows readily from seed and can become a troublesome weed in old woodland.

Properties and traditional uses

Holly wood is the whitest of all woods, and is heavy, hard and fine-grained. It can be stained and polished and is used to make furniture or in engraving work. It is commonly used to make walking sticks. Holly wood also makes good firewood and burns with a strong heat. Holly is valuable for nature providing dense cover for birds and small mammals, nectar and pollen for bees, and berries which are a vital source of food for mice and birds. Mistle thrushes will often fight to protect the berries on their favourite holly tree from other birds. Holly, with its colourful berries, has always been used as a decoration in the winter and there are now numerous variegated forms to add to their ornamental value.

Description

Wild privet is a semi-evergreen shrub of hedgerows, woodland edges and grassland scrub. It can grow to a height of 3 m. It is identified by its small, oval, glossy, green leaves and smooth bark.

WTML Steven Kind

Clusters of small, fragrant, white flowers appear at the ends of its twigs, and matt-black berries appear in the autumn.

Natural occurrence

Wild privet grows all over the British Isles except for the Highlands and Flow Country of Scotland. In Ireland it is an introduced species and largely confined to planted field hedges. It occurs in most areas of Hertfordshire, the exception being the more strongly acidic gravels and clays in the central and southern areas.

Properties and traditional uses

Privet is valuable for wildlife and, although the black berries are poisonous to humans, they are readily eaten by thrushes and other birds. The privet widely used for hedging in gardens is not our native privet, but is *Ligustrum ovalifolium*, also known as Korean privet. It keeps its leaves better through the winter.

Yew
Taxus baccata

Description
Yew is a medium height (15 m) evergreen tree with dark green, pointed needles for foliage. Yew trees are generally dioecious, i.e. have male and female flowers on separate trees, though they can

Colin Legg

Donato Cinicolo

occasionally change sex. Male flowers are small but numerous producing clouds of pollen; female flowers are white and bud-like. The fruit, unlike most other conifers, is a single seed enclosed in a red fleshy berry.

Natural occurrence
Yew trees occur in all parts of the British Isles except the Highlands and Flow Country of Scotland. Their distribution in Ireland is somewhat more scattered, but note that the "Irish Yew" is not a separate species but is thought to be a mutant form of the common yew. Yew is widespread throughout Hertfordshire, many having been planted and others self-sown from seed.

Properties and traditional uses
Yew timber is rich orange-brown in colour, closely grained and incredibly strong and durable. Traditionally the wood was used to make long bows and tool handles. A yew spear head, found in 1911 at Clacton-on-sea, is estimated to be more than 300,000 years old. Yew is used for topiary and hedging in parks and gardens. All parts of the yew tree, except the fleshy fruit, contain poisonous alkaloids. Yew clippings are collected and taxanes extracted for use in a drug for combating lung and prostate cancer.

Guelder rose
Viburnum opulus

Description
Guelder rose is a large (5 m) and beautiful shrub. Leaves are three-lobed with coarse, serrated edges and a rounded base.

Linda McArdell

In spring, the leaves are green, and they change to orange-yellow or red in autumn. The flowers are creamy white and come in flat topped inflorescences. The bright red, translucent berries hang in bunches.

Natural occurrence
Guelder rose can be found throughout the British Isles, except for the Highlands and Flow Country of Scotland. It grows throughout Hertfordshire, but most commonly on the damper soils in the north-east and west.

Properties and traditional uses
Guelder rose is commonly grown in parks and gardens where it is valued for its flowers, berries and autumn colour.

Dogwood
Cornus sanguinea

Gorse
Ulex europaeus

> The origin of the name comes from the smooth straight twigs, which were used to make butchers' skewers. Skewers used to be called 'dags' or 'dogs', so the name means 'skewer wood'.

Description

Dogwood is a medium-sized (3 m) shrub, though occasionally grows to more than double this height. Twigs are bright crimson in the sunlight, or lime green when in the shade. Leaves are fresh green, oval, and 6 cm long,  with smooth sides and characteristic curving veins. They fade to a rich crimson colour before falling in autumn. Small creamy white flowers are followed by small black berries. If leaves are pulled apart they reveal a stringy latex-like substance.

Kate Bretherton

Natural occurrence

Dogwood is found all over England and Wales, but only rarely in Scotland and Ireland. In Hertfordshire dogwood is a common shrub, characteristic of hedgerows, scrub and coppice woodlands.

Properties and traditional uses

Dogwood is commonly used as an ornamental plant in gardens, where it is used to provide autumn colour. The many cultivated varieties provide a dazzling display of coloured stems in the winter.

Description

Gorse is a small (2.5 m) evergreen shrub covered in scale-like leaves, needle-sharp spines and distinctive, coconut-perfumed yellow flowers. It generally blooms from January to June, though it may flower sporadically throughout the year. There are also two species of dwarf gorse, *Ulex gallii*, which grows in the west of England and Wales, and *Ulex minor*, which is confined to southeast England.

Natural occurrence

Gorse is common throughout the British Isles. It is found in central, west and south Hertfordshire. Most are probably derived from introduced plants, though it is thought that those on Nomansland Common might be native to the County.

Properties and traditional uses

Gorse is an important shrub as it provides shelter and food for many insects and birds, such as Dartford Warblers, Stonechats and Yellowhammers. However, it can quickly become invasive, forming dense, impenetrable stands.

Heartwood giants

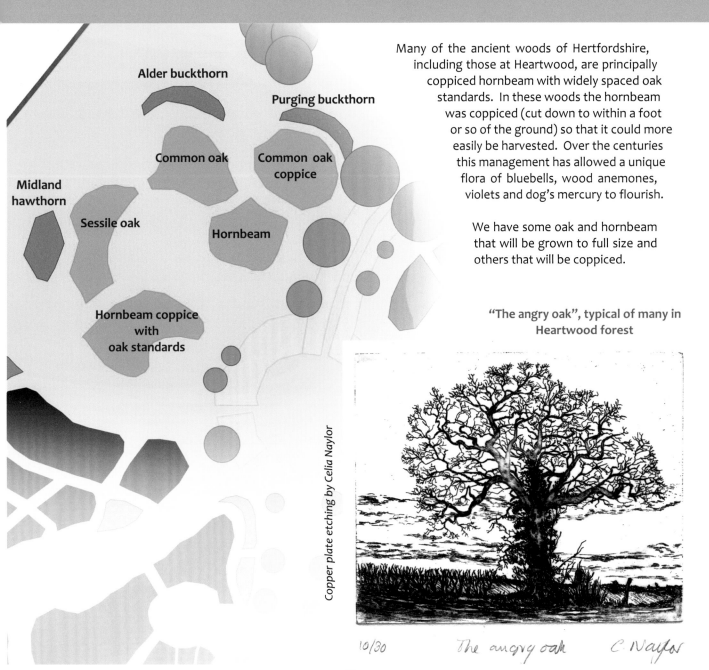

Alder buckthorn

Purging buckthorn

Common oak

Common oak coppice

Midland hawthorn

Sessile oak

Hornbeam

Hornbeam coppice with oak standards

Many of the ancient woods of Hertfordshire, including those at Heartwood, are principally coppiced hornbeam with widely spaced oak standards. In these woods the hornbeam was coppiced (cut down to within a foot or so of the ground) so that it could more easily be harvested. Over the centuries this management has allowed a unique flora of bluebells, wood anemones, violets and dog's mercury to flourish.

We have some oak and hornbeam that will be grown to full size and others that will be coppiced.

"The angry oak", typical of many in Heartwood forest

Copper plate etching by Celia Naylor

10/30   The angry oak   C. Naylor

41

Common oak
Quercus robur

Description

The common, or English, oak is arguably the best known and loved of British native trees. It can grow to an immense size (35 m), with broad and spreading crown and sturdy branches.

Leaves are around 10 cm long with four to five deep lobes with smooth edges. They are connected to the twig by a very short stalk. Male flowers are long yellow hanging catkins, which distribute pollen into the air. Female flowers are tiny and red, and the acorns that follow are

formed in cups borne on a long stalk, or peduncle, giving common oak its alternative name of pedunculate oak. One day our small oak saplings will grow into majestic giants.

Oak coppice. An oak tree takes up to 150 years to mature, and is then very difficult to fell and saw into planks. The alternative is to coppice and harvest the oak at regular intervals providing stems that are easier to harvest and ideal for producing round wood for construction or fuel. Our coppice plots will be cut back after about five years and then be coppiced every 15 to 20 years.

Natural occurrence

Oak, including both species, is the commonest native tree in the British Isles and it is ubiquitous. Oak is a dominant tree In Hertfordshire, and there are many large and ancient trees.

Properties and traditional uses

Oaks produce one of the hardest and most durable timbers on the planet, even its Latin name, *Quercus robur*, means strength. However, it takes up to 150 years before an oak is ready to use in construction. It has been a prized hardwood timber for thousands of years, was the primary ship building material until the mid-19th century and remains a popular wood for architectural beams. Modern uses of English oak include flooring, wine barrels and firewood.

In the arboretum we have planted saplings at a close 1.5 m spacing so that competition will cause them to grow straight up in competition for light. This is how they are grown as a timber crop. Tannin found in the bark has been used to tan leather since at least Roman times.

Oak trees frequently form galls as a reaction to a parasitic wasp attack, and these were used for centuries to make oak gall ink. It is among the most permanent inks known, and was used for the Magna Carta (1215) and the Domesday Book (1086). These documents are still legible today.

Oak forests provide a rich biodiverse habitat supporting more life forms than any other native trees. They host hundreds of species of insect, supplying many British birds with an important food source. In autumn mammals, such as badgers and deer take advantage of the falling acorns.

Sessile oak
Quercus petraea

Description
Sessile oak grows to be a large (30 m) tree. It is very similar to common oak in most respects, but has a more upright trunk and straighter branches. The leaves have more lobes and longer stalks than those of the common oak and, decisively, the acorn cups have very short stalks.

Natural occurrence
Sessile oak occurs throughout the British Isles, with the exception of central Ireland and some parts of East Anglia. It is far less frequent than the common oak in Hertfordshire, and it is thought that the ones we have were planted for timber in the late 18th and early 19th centuries.

Male catkins

Properties and traditional uses
Sessile oak has the same properties and usage as common oak, and it also supports a very rich biodiversity providing food for no less than 280 species of insect and all the birds and other predators that feed on the insects.

Hornbeam
Carpinus betulus

Description
Hornbeam is a large (25 m) tree with pale grey bark marked with wavy vertical lines. Leaves are of similar shape to beech leaves but are smaller, have serrated edges and are more deeply furrowed.

Ruari Burnett

They become golden yellow to orange before falling in autumn. Each tree bears male and female catkins and after pollination by wind, female catkins develop into papery, green winged fruits. The name probably comes from old English in which "horn beam" means hard tree.

Natural occurrence
Hornbeam grows throughout England, Wales and southern Scotland, but is rare elsewhere. It is common throughout Hertfordshire except in the extreme northeast. Its strongholds are the numerous old hornbeam coppices with standards.

Properties and traditional uses
Hornbeam timber is extremely hard and strong, so was mainly used for furniture and flooring. Traditional uses included ox-yokes, butchers' chopping blocks and cogs for windmills and water mills. Hornbeam burns well and makes good firewood and charcoal. The hornbeam coppice at Heartwood was probably harvested to provide fuel for London.

Ancient coppiced hornbeam in Langley wood, Heartwood Forest

Ornamental shrubs in this section

Alder buckthorn
Frangula alnus

Purging buckthorn
Rhamnus cathartica

Midland hawthorn
Crataegus laevigata

Description

These two related species form small (5-6 m) trees or shrubs, with purging buckthorn (often known simply as "buckthorn") being spiny and bearing small black poisonous berries in the autumn. Alder buckthorn is free from thorns and has green berries that ripen to red and eventually dark purple or black. The leaves are similar, though are alternate on alder buckthorn and opposite on the stems of purging buckthorn.

Alder buckthorn

Purging buckthorn

Natural occurrence

Both species occur predominantly in central and southern England though purging buckthorn appears to be absent from the southwest. In Hertfordshire, purging buckthorn is widespread in hedgerows and scrub, most abundant on chalky soils but also found elsewhere. Alder buckthorn is rare, though has been planted in wet areas and as an amenity shrub.

Properties and traditional uses

Traditionally the fruits, leaves and bark of both buckthorns were used to make yellow, green, blue and grey dyes. Both were once used as a purgative, hence the name of purging buckthorn. Alder buckthorn charcoal was prized in the manufacture of gunpowder, and was regarded as the best wood for time fuses because it has a very even burn rate. Both buckthorns are valuable for wildlife and are the only food plant of caterpillars of the brimstone butterfly.

Description

Midland hawthorn is a small (8 m) tree or large dense, thorny shrub. The leaves have three broad lobes, as opposed to the

narrower and deeper lobes of common hawthorn. It flowers a couple of weeks earlier than common hawthorn. The flowers are usually creamy white, but are occasionally pink or red. They have two stigmas and are followed by haws that contain two seeds.

Nature Photographers Ltd/WTML

Natural occurrence

Midland hawthorn occurs in central and southeast England, but rarely elsewhere. In Hertfordshire it is found widely in ancient and semi-natural woodland, old hedgerows, and mature scrub.

Properties and traditional uses

It is often planted as hedging in wildlife gardens as its heavy thickets provide good shelter and effective screens. Most of the ornamental hawthorns with colourful blossom have been derived, at least in part, from the Midland hawthorn.

Royal Horticultural Society (RHS) list of native trees and shrubs

This is the full list of native trees and shrubs published by the RHS. Those in the arboretum are shown in **bold**.

Large trees

		Height m	page
Alder	*Alnus glutinosa*	25	26
Ash	*Fraxinus excelsior*	30	35
Beech	*Fagus sylvatica*	25	31
Birch, silver	*Betula pendula*	25	34
Elm, English	*Ulmus procera*	40	32
Elm, Huntingdon	*Ulmus x vegeta*	35	33
Elm, small-leaved	*Ulmus minor*	30	33
Elm, wych	*Ulmus glabra*	35	33
Elm, Plot's	*Ulmus plotii*	30	
Holly	*Ilex aquifolium*	25	38
Hornbeam	*Carpinus betulus*	25	43
Lime, large-leaved	*Tillia platyphyllos*	30	23
Lime, small-leaved	*Tilia cordata*	25	23
Oak, common	*Quercus robur*	35	42
Oak, sessile	*Quercus petraea*	30	43
Pine, Scots	*Pinus sylvestris*	30	31
Poplar, black	*Populus nigra*	35	9
Willow, crack	*Salix fragilis*	20	9
Willow, cricket bat	*Salix alba* var. *Caerulea*	20	8
Willow, white	*Salix alba*	25	8

Medium trees

		Height m	page
Aspen	*Populus tremula*	20	35
Birch, downy	*Betula pubescens*	20	34
Cherry, bird	*Prunus padus*	15	17
Cherry, wild	*Prunus avium*	20	17
Hawthorn	*Crataegus monogyna*	10	25
Rowan	*Sorbus aucuparia*	15	19
Service, wild	*Sorbus torminalis*	20	19
Whitebeam	*Sorbus aria*	20	36
Whitebeam, Devon	*Sorbus devoniensis*	13	37
Whitebeam	3 other rare species		
Willow, almond	*Salix triandra*	10	13
Willow, bay	*Salix pentandra*	10	12
Willow, goat	*Salix caprea*	10	11
Yew	*Taxus baccata*	15	39

Small trees

		Height m	page
Blackthorn	*Prunus spinosa*	5	21
Box	*Buxus sempervirens*	5	24
Buckthorn, alder	*Frangula alnus*	5	44
Crab apple	*Malus sylvestris*	9	18
Elder	*Sambucus nigra*	6	21
Field maple	*Acer campestre*	8	25
Hawthorn, midland	*Crataegus laevigata*	8	44
Hazel	*Corylus avellana*	5	20 & 24
Pear, Plymouth	*Pyrus cordata*	8	16
Service-tree, Arran	*Sorbus pseudofennica*	7	37
Strawberry tree	*Arbutus unedo*	8	16
Whitebeam, Arran	*Sorbus arranensis*	8	37
Whitebeam	7 other rare species		
Willow, grey	*Salix cinerea*	6	11
Willow, osier	*Salix viminalis*	6	12

Large shrubs

		Height m	page
Buckthorn, purging	*Rhamnus cathartica*	6	44
Dogwood	*Cornus sanguinea*	3	40
Guelder rose	*Viburnum opulus*	5	39
Juniper	*Juniperus communis*	6	18
Privet, wild	*Ligustrum vulgare*	3	38
Rose, dog	*Rosa canina*	4	29
Rose	6 other species		
Sea buckthorn	*Hippophae rhamnoides*	6	20
Spindle	*Euonymus europaeus*	3	26
Wayfaring tree	*Viburnum lantana*	5	27
Whitebeam	3 rare species		
Willow, dark-leaved	*Salix myrsinifolia*	4	14
Willow, eared	*Salix aurita*	3	14
Willow, purple	*Salix purpurea*	5	13
Willow, tea-leaved	*Salix phylicifolia*	4	14

Medium and small shrubs

		Height m	page
Briar, sweet	*Rosa rubiginosa*	2.5	29
Broom	*Cytisus scoparius*	1.5	27
Gorse	*Ulex europaeus*	2.5	40
Gorse, western	*Ulex galii*	2	
Rose, field	*Rosa arvensis*	2	28
Rose	3 other species		
Rose, burnet	*Rosa spinosissima*	1	28
Butcher's broom	*Ruscus aculeatus*	0.75	

Acknowledgements

Louise Neicho, Woodland Trust Site Manager (Central England).
Simon Toomer, Director of the Westonbirt National Arboretum.
Richard Gornall, Director of the Leicester University Botanic Garden and Attenborough Arboretum.
Robert Somerville. For information on the current state of British woodlands and their uses.
Rachel Lee for giving generous access to photos in the Woodland Trust Media Library.
Tim Wright, Colin and Keren Beazley, Steve Parkes and Colin Legg for botanical, artistic and editorial advice.

Web sites
National Biodiversity Network's Atlas: https://nbnatlas.org/
      used for correct names and for distribution in the British Isles.
Woodland Trust for information on many of the trees and shrubs.

Various other web sites including:
    naturespot.org.uk
    native-scottish-trees.org.uk
    wildlifetrusts.org
    bsbi.org (Botanical Society of Britain and Ireland)

References
Trevor J James. (2009) *Flora of Hertfordshire*.   Hertfordshire Natural History Society.
Simon Toomer. (2010) *Planting and Maintaining a Tree Collection*. Timber Press.
Piers Warren. (2006) *British Native Trees. Their past and present uses*. Wildeye.

Photos
Photos without acknowledgement were taken by the author. All others show the photographer's name.
Photos with the credit WTML have been provided from the Woodland Trust Media Library.

Line drawings
Created and supplied by Celia Naylor.

Maps
Prepared by the author using his own surveys superimposed on an OS map reproduced by permission of Ordnance Survey on behalf of HMSO. © Crown copyright and database right 2012. All rights reserved. Ordnance Survey licence number 100021607.
All maps have north at the top.